For Karen —

Prepare Your Heart and be a

Great Mom

Blessings!

Maria
Rodgers

*Moms: Prepare your hearts for the moments
hidden in the minutes of your life!*

Visit www.Great MomBook.com for a free Meeting Kit from *Prepare Your Heart* author, Maria Rodgers O'Rourke. It's an easy and inexpensive way to feature a great speaker at your next mothers' group meeting. The kit includes a video presentation, meeting agenda and more! Free for individuals, too!

Prepare Your Heart and be a
Great Mom

By: Maria Rodgers O'Rourke

MRO Communications, Inc., Publisher

© 2009 by Maria Rodgers O'Rourke
All rights reserved. No part of this publication may be reproduced, stored in a retrieval system, or transmitted in any form or by any means, electronic, mechanical, recording or otherwise—except by a reviewer who may quote brief passages in a review to be printed in a magazine, newspaper, or on the Web—without the prior written permission of MRO Communications, Inc., 1602 Fontana Drive, St. Louis, MO 63146. Printed in Canada.

ISBN 13: 978-0-9800227-1-1

ISBN 10: 0-9800227-1-1

Library of Congress Control Number: 2009900978

The scripture quotations contained herein are from the New Revised Standard Version Bible: Catholic Edition, copyright © 1989, by the Division of Christian Education of the National Council of the Churches of Christ in the U.S.A. Used by permission. All rights reserved.

To my dear mother-in-law, Doris, who left this world brighter, greener, and better decorated than she found it!

Preface

All moms hope and pray for the health and happiness of their children. Yet, truth be told, most moms hold another deep desire: That their children will say they are good, even great, moms.

In the quest to be a great mom, she compares herself to other moms: friends, neighbors, the moms at school and, most profoundly, her own mother.

But seeking the title of "great mom" outside oneself is really a futile effort. To be a great mom, the answer is so simple, and yet life-changing—to be a great mom she must lead with her heart.

There are many clichés about the heart—heart-to-heart talks, getting to the heart of the matter, how do you mend a broken heart?—all of which touch on the extraordinary experience of motherhood. Elizabeth Stone has said that being a mom is like having a piece of your heart walking around outside yourself. Moms understand the sweet pain that comes with this reality. Mom's life is a balancing act of planning and spontaneity, feast and famine, sickness and health, laughter and tears. All of it mixed together and rolled out every day as she pours her heart into being a great mom.

With each new day, moms recommit to the sacred and sometimes scary duties of motherhood. In my experience, and with many women I talk to, we tend to let tasks and activities set the agenda for our day. In order to lead with our hearts, we need to take a deep breath every day and put time with God at the top of our list. When we do, we'll discover the moments hidden in the minutes of our lives.

This book's simple formula is designed to help moms take the time they need, every day, to prepare their hearts and be a great mom.

How to use Prepare Your Heart and be a Great Mom

The reflections begin on a Sunday of your choice, and follow along for a total of four weeks.

Each day, find a quiet place and take a few deep breaths. Read the day's reflection, and ponder the words and phrases that strike you. Then, turn to the facing journal page and answer the questions listed there. The questions are the same every day, but your answers will vary. Here are some examples:

- Today I am grateful for … (A simple list will do: my home, my health, a warm cup of coffee, sunshine, etc.)
- My intentions for today … (Example: to appreciate my child's energy, to be kind to all whom I meet, to be patient in traffic)
- My to-do list for today includes … (Whatever tasks you have on your mind or need to accomplish)

At the end of each week, there are two extra journal pages for a mini-retreat. They include questions to reflect on the week past and to create a vision for the week ahead.

This book is your book; go ahead and write in it! Carry it with you throughout the day, crossing off your to-do list and rereading your gratitude list and intention statement. Try this: Partner with a friend as you read and journal—check in with each other every day and share your insights. Use this book to help you lead with your heart during your hectic day.

Sunday, Week One

A new heart I will give you, and a new spirit I will put within you; and I will remove from your body the heart of stone and give you a heart of flesh.
Ezekiel 36:25

Motherhood changes everything.

When we raise a child, our vision of life expands and deepens to include and focus on this other new life that has appeared where one did not exist before. Our lives become forever parsed in two—before the baby, and after. Our hearts are filling and overflowing with love, delight, and joy at this new person. We love more deeply, profoundly, and completely than we ever imagined we could.

Any part of the heart petrified by regrets or grudges is softened with the hope of new life, new beginnings, and new possibilities that is enfleshed in this new being. Somehow, by God's grace, as this child's mother you will share in this new life, too.

Today we begin our daily gratitude practice. Listing who and what we're thankful for has the power to transform our outlook on life. Doing it daily will open our eyes to even more blessings. Using the space on the next page, begin your gratitude practice today.

today I am grateful for

my intentions for the day

my to-do list for today

Monday, Week One

> *My brothers and sisters whenever you face trials of any kind,*
> *consider it nothing but joy.*
> *James 1:2*

Trials and tribulations are a staple of the mom's life. Our days are filled with care and concern for our offspring, and our thoughts are split between our children, our work, and our needs.

But would we have it any other way? Our children bring spontaneity, laughter, and joy into our lives. So instead of fretting over the trials, let's give thanks for the instigators of them … and for having been entrusted with their care and upbringing.

My mother-in-law tells a wonderful story of when her daughter, the youngest of five and the only girl, came crying to her, imploring, "Mommy, tell the boys to stop teasing me so much!" She replied, "Why, honey, they only tease you because they love you so much." Her child contemplated this response for a moment and said, "Then tell 'em to stop loving me so much!"

Think of a time when your child was driving you crazy. Looking back, is there something about the situation that makes you laugh?

today I am grateful for

my intentions for the day

my to-do list for today

Tuesday, Week One

> *Every generous act of giving, with every perfect gift, is from above, coming down from the Father of lights, with whom there is no variation or shadow.*
> *James 1:17*

One way we grow in caring for children is in becoming a selfless giver. The helpless being placed in our arms needs constant care, and we sacrifice comfort, sleep, and personal hygiene to provide it. Even as our children grow and need less physical support, they still command from us our mental and emotional presence.

Here's how my mornings tend to go. I wake up, or the alarm goes off, and as I drift out of sleep my mind kicks in and begins ruminating over all that must be attended to this day. As the thoughts run through my head, my body stiffens with tension and anxiety and soon my whole being is driven up and out of bed and head first into the tasks of the day: get the kids off to school; get ready for work; does the trash go out today?; Mom, I need lunch money; we're out of milk; the jeans in the dryer are still wet; who used all the hot water?; where did I put the checkbook?; I need a haircut; the dog took a poop in the basement. I need a break before I've left the house!

We aren't alone in this giving. We are joining forces with God, the source of all goodness, to provide for our children. In our love for them, God's presence in our world is made manifest. But be sure to grab a nap now and then!

today I am grateful for

my intentions for the day

my to-do list for today

Wednesday, Week One

You must understand this, my beloved: let everyone be quick to listen, slow to speak and slow to anger.
James 1:19

Whoa! This is a tough one where mothering is concerned. The kids will create messes that need to be cleaned, pierce our hearts with their criticism, and make choices in life that appear crazy at best and self-destructive at worst.

When commiserating with my siblings about the challenges of parenting, we often wish we could download all our personal experience into our children's minds and hearts, so they might start out further along than we did, and that our hard-won lessons might benefit them. Instead, we're left with setting boundaries, loving, and watching them learn from their own bumps and bruises. We have the opportunity to first listen to them, to be slow to offer our input or opinion, and even slower in our anger (also known as judgment) of what we hear.

First, we love. We open our hearts to the unique beauty of this person we've co-created with God, love them for who they are, and do not condemn them for not being who we thought they should be. When we love them for *who* they are, God's grace can enter in and transform (where needed) *what* they are.

today I am grateful for

my intentions for the day

my to-do list for today

Thursday, Week One

> *God said, "this is the sign of the covenant that I make between me and you and every living creature that is with you, for all future generations: I have set my bow in the clouds and it shall be a sign of the covenant between me and the earth."*
> *Genesis 8:12-13*

A covenant is distinct from a contract in that a contract is based on living up to stated expectations while a covenant is based on relationship and love. God's invitation to a covenant relationship is symbolized in the rainbow following the great flood; all of God's creation is beloved to him.

Ideally, families are rooted in covenant love, but we need a few contracts to keep things running smoothly. Our dinnertime rule is: if you don't eat your whole dinner, you don't get any snacks. One particular night she felt so strongly about not eating her corn that when reminded of the rule, she conceded the point and left the vegetables to cool on her plate.

On the counter, there was a nearly empty bag of chips. My daughter picked up the bag and put some in her mouth. I raised a finger and said, "Uh-uh [no]!" She immediately dashed to the trash can, opened her mouth and pushed the chips on her tongue into the can.

Instantly, I scooped her into my arms, kissing her and praising her honesty. My heart was overflowing love for this child who had just tested the limits of my patience!

God helps moms love first and enforce the rules later. The constant is love, no matter what.

today I am grateful for

my intentions for the day

my to-do list for today

Friday, Week One

> *You see that faith was active along with his works, and faith was brought to completion in his works.*
> *James 2:22*

Faith and action go hand in hand. In this book of the Bible, James laments those who are of great faith and yet do not reach out to help others, and also those who do good deeds without the love to back up the deeds.

Mother Teresa said we are not called to do great things, but to do small things with great love. Mom's work includes many small, seemingly insignificant tasks—"other duties as required," the job description might say. Yet those small things, when done with great love, can be the means by which those around us know the love of God. No task is too small if it is done with honor and love for the person who benefits from the act.

As you go about the many small tasks that make up your day, pause before each and think for a moment about the person or people who will be served by it. Whisper a quick prayer for them as you perform that task.

today I am grateful for

my intentions for the day

my to-do list for today

Saturday, Week One

Reflections for Week One's Mini-Retreat

Give yourself about 30 minutes alone to complete the following questions:

Review the week's reflections. Any new insights? How did the reflections impact your week?

Are there any new blessings in your life this week? Who or what are they?

Write down one statement of faith or intention that you take with you from this week. For example: "I believe God's abundant love is at work in me and my family." "I will listen to those I love before speaking."

Write your statement on a few sticky notes and put them in three places you see every day: mirror, refrigerator, wallet.

What gift can you give yourself this weekend? Time with a friend? Read a chapter of a good book? Go to a movie? Get a massage? Go for a walk?

Celebrate the past week, and look to the coming one: What are some things you'll do differently this coming week? What's working for you? Write down a few of your intentions.

Sunday, Week Two

> *For all who are led by the Spirit are children of God. For you did not receive a spirit of slavery to fall back into fear, but you have received a spirit of adoption. When we cry "Abba!" "Father!" it is that very spirit bearing witness with our spirit that we are children of God, and if children, then heirs, heirs of God and joint heirs with Christ.*
> *Romans 8:14-17*

As a mom, I started this job thinking I needed to have all the answers; now I see how I can help my children find their own.

"Drama" describes episodes of teenage social turbulence. My daughter has had her share.

Fortunately, during one episode, she confided in me. I vacillated between wanting to fix the situation for her and letting her work it out on her own. Over time, I've learned to simply listen and relate to her feelings. I have come to trust her to figure out the right thing to do; she just needs help to get through the feelings and see her way to an answer. By really listening to her, she knows I have confidence in her. As the drama cloud lifted, we both experienced the blessed lightness of reconciliation and release.

This new approach does not come at the expense of guidance and rules. Rather, it acknowledges that both my child and I are growing; with each life experience we share, there are opportunities for all of us to learn. In the process, I've experienced the Divine Providence that wills goodness for all members of my family. It is God's greatest desire that we each live to the fullest expression of the talents and gifts he's given us, and he'll use our family dynamics to bring this vision into reality.

today I am grateful for

my intentions for the day

my to-do list for today

Monday, Week Two

> *But the Lord answered her, "Martha, Martha, you are worried and distracted by many things; there is need of only one thing. Mary has chosen the better part, which will not be taken away from her."*
> Luke 10:41-42

Let's rewind a bit and take a look at the scene that took place before Jesus' remark to Martha. When we first met Martha, she was running around her house hosting Jesus and his disciples. In her whirlwind of activity, she noticed her sister, Mary, had seated herself at the foot of Jesus and was enjoying his teaching. Noting Jesus' hold on Mary's attention, Martha asked him to intercede with Mary and ask her to contribute to the work of entertaining their guests. Instead, Jesus turns his rebuke to Martha, and seems to judge her efforts as unimportant.

How hurtful and confusing! Imagine the sting of embarrassment in her heart, the flush of red on her cheeks, and the tears that filled her eyes as she turned away from Jesus.

My heart goes out to Martha, for I too am "worried and distracted by many things," particularly when I'm hosting a party. If I could hear Jesus' tone of voice as he spoke to Martha, perhaps his words were spoken with compassion. Maybe he was inviting her to relax a bit and enjoy the fellowship of the gathering, and not let the tasks of entertaining consume her. Rather than a rebuke, these words are good advice to those of us who recall parties we host and remember how hard we worked and how little so-and-so did to help!

today I am grateful for

my intentions for the day

my to-do list for today

Tuesday, Week Two

> *Martha said to Jesus, "Lord, if you had been here, my brother would not have died. But even now I know that God will give you whatever you ask of him."*
> *John 11:21-22*

Fast-forward a few years and we meet a woman transformed by faith, evidenced in this "aha moment" for Martha. Jesus loved Martha, Mary, and their brother Lazarus very much. When Lazarus died, Jesus came to visit the sisters, and Martha met him on the road and proclaimed her faith in him. So there is hope for those of us who are busy about many things in life!

This story has yet another layer, touching on the essence of our relationship with God. Throughout the gospels, Jesus is repeatedly confronted with people in need of healing. It must have been clear to him what the condition was, yet in nearly every circumstance he asks, "What do you want me to do for you?" The person's response is as much a statement of the obvious as it is a declaration of faith. In a phrase as simple as, "I want to see (or walk, or be made clean)," they are in fact saying, "I believe you can heal me!" After the healing, Jesus' usual response was, "Your faith has cured you."

So it is with Martha. The one busy and distracted by many things becomes the one to declare her faith so simply and plainly that Jesus performs one of the most powerful and dramatic miracles of his ministry. Her faith healed her brother, and her family. If Martha can be so changed, there is hope for all the Martha's in the world!

today I am grateful for

my intentions for the day

my to-do list for today

Wednesday, Week Two

Draw near to God, and he will draw near to you.
James 4:8

I am not a morning person. My husband, co-workers, and friends will all verify this fact. That's why ten years ago a Lenten resolution to pray every morning was no small promise for me.

For the first few days, it was easy. I enthusiastically climbed out from under the warm covers each morning 45 minutes earlier than usual with a bit of self-satisfaction that I was able to make this sacrifice for God. Later, as the days turned into weeks, it was more and more difficult to rise so early. That was when the sacrifice really began. I didn't feel so self-satisfied on the days when our warm bed was more appealing to me than the day's scripture and my morning tea. There were some mornings when I did choose to stay tucked in. The extra sleep I got, however, was never very restful.

A priest friend of mine encouraged me by saying that God would send special graces to help me keep my promise. The grace came in ways I never expected, such as spontaneously waking up just minutes before the alarm went off. Or when a passage from the day's scripture applied so well to a situation in my life, I knew God was very present in our morning meetings. These comforts kept me going, and this Lenten practice changed my life in many ways. What are some graces that are appearing for you during these days of reflection and gratitude?

today I am grateful for

my intentions for the day

my to-do list for today

Thursday, Week Two

*Wisdom teaches her children and gives help to those who seek her.
Whoever loves her loves life and…are filled with joy.
Sirach 4:11-12*

After Easter, I'd like to say I continued my morning prayer habit throughout the year, but such was not the case. A busy life and my weak flesh were not supportive of the prayer my willing spirit desired. God continued to send his grace, however, and in a most unexpected form: my first child. God gave her life during that special Lenten season.

While pregnant, I was assured by friends and family alike that I'd never again know a good night's sleep. They were right. In the early days, she was up two and three times a night. By the following Lent, she was sleeping through the night, but like any mother, I was awakened by her coos and coughs at all hours. When I began anew my Lenten pledge of daily prayer, she'd often make a few sounds about 45 minutes before I needed to wake up. This was the gentle nudge I needed to get up and pray … a special grace sent to help me live up to my promise.

today I am grateful for

my intentions for the day

my to-do list for today

Friday, Week Two

> *Do not delay to turn back to the Lord, and do not
> postpone it from day to day.*
> Sirach 5:7

A familiar refrain for tired moms is "maybe tomorrow." Our days are so hectic and full—we intend to get so much done, and the time slips away, or a little one gets sick, or the car breaks down, or everyone's hungry—and before we know it the day is gone and we fall into bed, exhausted.

Our scripture today reminds us of the attention our relationship with God needs. "Maybe tomorrow" you'll have time to pray, but make time today. To paraphrase St. Ignatius Loyola: If you don't have one hour to pray every day, perhaps you should pray for two.

What are some of the blessings this daily quiet time has brought to your life? For me: my mornings go more smoothly; my gratitude list is easier to complete; and when setbacks arise during the day, I'm more likely to respond with humor or calm assurance that it will all work out. For these, I can trade a few extra minutes in bed!

today I am grateful for

_____

_____

my intentions for the day

_____

_____

_____

my to-do list for today

_____

_____

_____

_____

_____

_____

Saturday, Week Two

Reflections for Week Two's Mini-Retreat

Give yourself about 30 minutes alone to complete the following questions:

Review the week's reflections. Any new insights? How did the reflections impact your week?

Are there any new blessings in your life this week? Who or what are they?

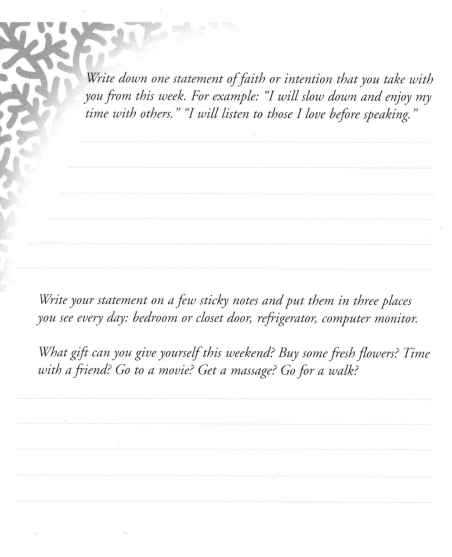

Write down one statement of faith or intention that you take with you from this week. For example: "I will slow down and enjoy my time with others." "I will listen to those I love before speaking."

Write your statement on a few sticky notes and put them in three places you see every day: bedroom or closet door, refrigerator, computer monitor.

What gift can you give yourself this weekend? Buy some fresh flowers? Time with a friend? Go to a movie? Get a massage? Go for a walk?

Celebrate the past week, and look to the coming one: What are some things you'll do differently this coming week? What's working for you? Write down a few of your intentions.

Sunday, Week Three

Can a woman forget her nursing child, or show no compassion for the child of her womb? Even these may forget, yet I [the Lord] will not forget you.
Isaiah 49:15

When my first-born child started high school, I happened to drive by the school during the first week of classes. I realized she was inside, and felt a sudden, strong connection to this building that had meant little to me just days earlier. I imagined her walking through the halls, finding her way to class, laughing with her friends. This young woman, once my tiny baby girl, was making her way on her own. It was, as Elizabeth Stone has written, like my heart was walking around outside my body.

Motherhood brings with it an intense love for one's child. Every mother I've ever met tells me that she never knew she could love someone as deeply as she loves her child.

This truth leads us to a profound experience of God's love for us. If, as the prophet Isaiah says, God loves us more than a mother loves her child, imagine the vastness of that love!

Today, take a deep breath and allow yourself to relax into it. Let God's arms fold gently around you, and feel God's warmth flooding your heart. Trust God's love to be generous enough to love you, and the parts of your heart walking around outside!

today I am grateful for

my intentions for the day

my to-do list for today

Monday, Week Three

Jesus fixed his gaze on them and said, "For man it is impossible, but not for God. With God all things are possible."
Mark 10:27

Gospel writer Mark gives us a wonderful bit of stage direction to begin our reflection. "Jesus fixed his gaze on them."

Close your eyes and imagine Jesus fixing his gaze on you—his tender, compassionate, earnest eyes focused on you, as if you were the most important to him in this moment—which of course you are.

Tell Jesus whatever is on your heart today—your hopes and joys, worries and sorrows. Speak to him the questions you hold deep in your heart, the unresolved longings to which your mind cannot fashion an answer. Let Jesus give you his answer:

"With God, all things are possible."

today I am grateful for

my intentions for the day

my to-do list for today

Tuesday, Week Three

You shall be holy, for I am holy.
1 Peter 1:10-16

The word "sacrifice" comes from the two words "sacred" and "to make." When we sacrifice, we forgo one thing for something else we feel is of greater value.

Moms are well acquainted with sacrifice. On New Year's Eve a few years ago, my daughter caught horrible stomach flu. She was violently ill, so much so that her most comfortable position was lying on the cool tile floor of our hall bathroom.

Through the night I stayed with her. My head, heavy with fatigue, rested on the wall behind me as I sat on the floor, my arm resting on her side. There was little I could do to relieve her pain, but I could sit with her. And so I did.

In that dark moment on a bathroom floor, I sacrificed sleep for the greater value of my daughter's comfort and assurance that she was not alone in a time of trial and pain.

God's grace gave me the strength to sit with her in the lonely dark hours of the night. Together, we loved her through the illness. With that small sacrifice, our human condition was made holy.

today I am grateful for

my intentions for the day

my to-do list for today

Wednesday, Week Three

> *Then Simeon blessed them and said to his mother, Mary,*
> *"This child is destined for the falling and the rising of many...and a*
> *sword will pierce your own soul, too."*
> *Luke 2:34-35*

Mothers know firsthand the sting of the many losses we experience in parenthood. Witnessing our child's physical pain, disappointments, and losses bring us great pain as well. Some moms hover too much, trying to protect their little ones from harm. But they're just fending off the inevitable bumps and bruises that are necessary for maturity.

Mary knew the joyous exultation of Jesus' birth, but Simeon's words brought home the truth that Jesus was created for more than her enjoyment. "Your children are not your own," the prophet tells us in Kahlil Gibran's book by that name. "You are the bows from which your children as living arrows are sent forth."

Our call as mothers is to guide, love, and then let go of our children. The pain may be great at times—unbearable in some circumstances—but it comes with the territory. As moms, we've turned ourselves over to the mystery of the life God has dreamt for our child's life. Ours is not to stand in the way or impose our ideas on this dream, but to facilitate it—perhaps even to the point of a sword piercing our hearts.

today I am grateful for

my intentions for the day

my to-do list for today

Thursday, Week Three

> *God searches out the abyss and the human heart; he understands [his holy ones'] innermost secrets.*
> Sirach 42:18

Have you ever received the perfect gift? Not one you hinted for, but one that fulfilled a deep desire, one that perhaps you hadn't spoken to anyone else? As I was growing up, my mother gave me such a gift every year.

My birthday is in December. Whenever I meet someone who also was born the same month, he or she will ask, "Don't you hate having it in December? Christmas and my birthday always got lumped together in my family."

Not true for me! I am blessed to have a mom who made each day special, and separate. Every year, Mom always made it clear that my birthday was for me, and that the gifts we exchanged on Christmas were in celebration of the Christ child's birth. As I matured, I came to understand Mom's perspective that our Christmas gift exchange wasn't just about the stuff we bought, but that it symbolized the greatest gift we give to each other—the gift of ourselves.

Mom's extra efforts for my birthday and for Christmas made me feel very special. Like God, she knew just what I wanted: to be loved.

today I am grateful for

my intentions for the day

my to-do list for today

Friday, Week Three

> *Come to me, all you that are weary and are carrying*
> *heavy burdens, and I will give you rest.*
> Matthew 11:28

I suspect most moms feel weary at least once a day. When I am close to collapsing under the heavy burdens of the daily care of my family, I remember the above passage, and my heart lifts.

There are tangible ways I feel the burden lifted, too. A couple of Christmases ago, my then-7-year-old did something remarkable. My husband was out of town on business, so I got a taste of single parent life as I juggled work, the house, and taking my kids to activities all week. Occasionally, I'll have an evening meeting. My teenager is used to this, but the younger one hates to see me go, especially during Christmastime. Our tree was up, but with only lights and no ornaments. In her excitement, the young one called me and asked permission to hang ornaments on the tree.

When I arrived home, the tree was a gorgeous sight! We snapped digital photos and sent them off to her dad right away.

Her initiative was a blessing in so many ways. As much as I love decorating the tree, I was delighted to cross that project off the list. Plus, my daughter had the wonderful sense of accomplishment and pride in a job well done and appreciated by her family. My young child took on the task and finished it with great style and *grace*. Come to think of it, that's her middle name!

today I am grateful for

my intentions for the day

my to-do list for today

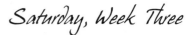

Saturday, Week Three

Reflections for Week Three's Mini-Retreat

Give yourself about 30 minutes alone to complete the following questions:

Review the week's reflections. Any new insights? How did the reflections impact your week?

Are there any new blessings in your life this week? Who or what are they?

Write down one statement of faith or intention that you take with you from this week. For example: "My life is filled with unexpected blessings." "All things are possible with God."

Write your statement on a few sticky notes and put them in three places you see every day: dashboard, refrigerator, checkbook cover.

What gift can you give yourself this weekend? Time with a friend? Fresh flowers? See a movie? A new outfit?

Celebrate the past week, and look to the coming one: What are some things you'll do differently this coming week? What's working for you? Write down a few of your intentions.

Sunday, Week Four

The Sabbath was made for humankind, and not humankind for the Sabbath.
Mark 2:27

Our daily Sabbath practice has just about become a habit—and it's one of the most important gifts we can give our family.

If you're ever feeling guilty for taking the time to read these reflections and complete these journal pages, I have three words for you: Get Over It!

This gift of time with God, the source of all love, you give yourself pays great dividends to all those you love. It's like when you travel by plane and the flight attendant instructs you to secure our own mask before you help the small child you're traveling with. In the event of an emergency, if you've passed out, who will look after your beloved child?

And so it is with our spiritual lives. Moms are entrusted with the spiritual care of their children, not only their bodies and minds. When we tend to our own faith, we're more tuned into God and better able to live out of that faith in our daily lives. We become a living testimonial to the power of God at work in transforming our lives—and our children cannot help but be influenced by this example.

today I am grateful for

my intentions for the day

my to-do list for today

Monday, Week Four

> *God's divine power has given us everything needed for life and godliness ...*
> *his precious and very great promises.*
> *2 Peter 1:3-4*

Imagine! The Creator of the Universe at work in your life, opening doors and calling you to greater good than you ever dreamed possible. Wow!

My husband and I waited a long time for our second child, years longer than we'd planned. The countless cycles that began in hope and ended in disappointment, coupled with hormonal assistance that drove me to the brink of depression, forced us to simply surrender and give up trying so hard.

Almost one year later, she was on the way. "Way to go!" my jubilant doctor proclaimed after the blood test. This girl, just like our first, arrived at exactly the right time.

We must remember—whether we wait in hope or rejoice in a dream realized, it all abides in God's divine power, which supplies all we need.

today I am grateful for

my intentions for the day

my to-do list for today

Tuesday, Week Four

Rejoice in hope, be patient in suffering, persevere in prayer.
Romans 12:12

Mothers are first-rate losers. Just ask any teenager you meet, including the one who lives with me.

When her first stinging retorts were lobbed at me, I sought the counsel of friends whose children were in their twenties. "Don't worry," they said. "She'll be back."

During that turbulent time, I rejoiced in the glimpses I caught of my sweet daughter, and learned to be patient when my feelings were hurt or we argued over homework or chores. Mostly, I learned to persevere in prayer—for deliverance from the current turmoil, or to be released from my desire to throttle my own flesh and blood. My deepest prayer was that she'd come through these days still deeply secure in her mother's love for her.

A dear priest friend of mine once wisely counseled me to ask God to "fill the gap" of love I encountered when my attempts at loving my daughter fell short of the ideal. Lord knows the size of that gap varied from day to day. I know God was, and continues to be, there to make up the difference between my limited human ability to love and God's perfect love for my daughter … and me.

today I am grateful for

my intentions for the day

my to-do list for today

Wednesday, Week Four

> *We know that all things work together for good for those who love God, who are called according to his purpose.*
> Romans 8:28

I came across a list of things to get done for a recent family event. I lost track of the list in my purse, so even though the event was past, the items on the list hadn't been checked off. For the fun of it, I went ahead and crossed out each item.

As I did, I recalled the anxiety that surrounded each item as I wrote it down. Now, with the event successfully behind me and my memories of a lovely day, the items on the list didn't seem so awful. In other words, what I'd been so worried about worked out well, in the end.

This is a lesson I want to take with me for every list I make from now on. As I write down each item, I'll trust that it will work out rather than worry that it won't. All things work together for good, scripture promises. Finding that old list in my purse was proof positive of just that!

today I am grateful for

my intentions for the day

my to-do list for today

Thursday, Week Four

*You shall love God with all your heart, and with all your soul
and with all your mind, and with all your strength.
You shall love your neighbor as yourself.
Mark 12:30-31*

My mother-in-law revealed her mystical self to me during her last weeks on earth. She was in the final stages of her battle with cancer, and one sunny day we took a brief walk and sat for a while on a fallen tree. She stared at the wood for a few moments, and with her delicate hand traced a circle around one spot. "See these beautiful shades of grey and brown?" she asked. The wood was spackled with a variety of colors, a multitude of shades only God could create. We sat quietly contemplating the wood for several seconds when she pointed and proclaimed, "That's the color I want to paint the kitchen!"

In today's scripture, Jesus teaches us the proper order of things in our life. My mother-in-law got it right: by recognizing the beauty in the wood, she loved God first. Then, her plan of action will carry that beauty into the world and bring joy to others. This is the divine instruction for moms—to love God with all our hearts, recognize his beauty in our lives, and share that beauty with those we love. Thanks, Doris!

today I am grateful for

my intentions for the day

my to-do list for today

Friday, Week Four

> *Let those who are friendly with you be many, but let
> your advisers be one in a thousand.*
> Sirach 6:6

Choose your friends wisely. Life has shown how fleeting some friendships can be. We can be hurt by someone we once considered a confidant. So while we will meet many people in a lifetime, only a small percentage will rate the title of best friend.

As we grow, we'll "try on" many friends, like clothing styles and make-up, to find the good fit, the one that feels most comfortable and safe. I've lost many friends along the way when we simply outgrew each other, or when the kids came along and we redefined "normal" in our lives. The enduring friendships have been the ones where love is constant, and without condition. I have so many in my life who expect and even demand my love; my dear friends should not be among these.

In seeking and heeding the advice of another, take to heart the wisdom of a friend who is living the life you want to live—one of integrity, honesty, deep happiness, love, and faith. When you find one like this, she is indeed a rare treasure.

today I am grateful for

my intentions for the day

my to-do list for today

Saturday, Week Four

Reflections for Week Four's Mini-Retreat

Give yourself about 30 minutes alone to complete the following questions:

Review the week's reflections. Any new insights? How did the reflections impact your week?

Are there any new blessings in your life this week? Who or what are they?

Write down one statement of faith or intention that you take with you from this week. For example: "I believe God's abundant love is at work in me and my family." "I will listen to those I love before speaking."

Write your statement on a few sticky notes and put them in three places you see every day: refrigerator, closet door, key ring.

What gift can you give yourself this weekend? New CD? Time with a friend? Read a chapter of a good book?

Celebrate the past week, and look to the coming one: What are some things you'll do differently this coming week? What's working for you? Write down a few of your intentions.

Additional Journal Pages

Acknowledgments

My deepest thanks to the people who helped bring this book into being: Lisa Hinrichs, Gail Kump, Christine Frank, and the many women who've laughed, commiserated, and cried with me over the challenges and blessings of motherhood. I am especially grateful to my own mother, my first role model, who showed me there's more to life than what our senses tell us, and to my husband, whose encouragement stretches me beyond my limitations. Most of all, to the two people who, on a daily basis, amaze, frustrate, and delight me—my daughters. Thanks for all you've taught me.

Prepare Your Heart and Be a Great Mom

To order books, meeting materials, and visit with other moms, visit **www.GreatMomBook.com**.

Maria Rodgers O'Rourke's heartfelt perspectives on motherhood and parenting make for popular presentations to women's organizations. Visit www.Great MomBook.com for a free Meeting Kit. It's an easy and inexpensive way to feature a great speaker at your next mothers' group meeting. The kit includes a video presentation and meeting agenda. Or, visit the website for more information on hosting Maria as speaker for your organization's next gathering!

Order more copies today! It's a great gift for the mom-to-be, or mothers of children of all ages.
Prepare Your Heart and Be a Great Mom is published by
MRO Communications, Inc.
1602 Fontana Drive, St. Louis, Missouri, 63146
Phone: 314-359-1942
Contact **info@GreatMomBook.com** for more information.
Also in the series: *Prepare Your Heart for a Great Christmas*